A Selection of Old-Time Recipes for Fudge

by

Various

Contents

British Library Cataloguing-in-Publication Data
A catalogue record for this book is available from
the British Library

ALL SORTS OF FUDGES

"I am glad that my Adonis hath a sweet tooth in his head"

ALOHA FUDGE

1 lb. (2 cups) brown sugar
1½ gills (¾ cup) milk
1 oz. (2 tablespoonfuls) butter

2 ozs. unsweetened chocolate
1 teaspoonful vanilla extract
½ teaspoonful rose extract

Put the sugar, milk, butter, and chocolate into a saucepan and bring slowly to boiling-point; then boil, stirring all the time, to 240°, or until it forms a soft ball when tested in cold water.

Remove from the fire, add the extracts, and beat till creamy. Pour into buttered tins and mark into squares before it hardens.

ANGEL FOOD FUDGE

1 gill (½ cup) strained honey
1 gill (½ cup) water
2 whites of eggs
¼ lb. (1 cup) blanched and chopped almonds

2 teaspoonfuls orange-flower water
1 lb. (2 cups) sugar
Pinch cream of tartar

Put the sugar, honey, and water into a saucepan and stir until dissolved; then add the cream of tartar

1

and boil until it registers 254° by the thermometer, or until, when tried in cold water, it forms a hard ball.

Beat the whites of the eggs to a stiff froth; then pour the boiling syrup gradually over them, beating all the time.

Continue beating until it becomes stiff; then add the orange-flower water and the almonds.

Pour into buttered tins, and when cool mark into squares.

BAKED FRUIT FUDGE

½ lb. (1 cup) sugar	2 eggs
1 oz. (2 tablespoonfuls) butter	2 squares melted chocolate
1 teaspoonful lemon extract	2 ozs. (½ cup) flour
1 teaspoonful orange extract	2 ozs. (½ cup) shredded fruits
½ teaspoonful vanilla extract	

Scatter the fruit over a well-buttered tin. Cream the butter and sugar together, then add the yolks of the eggs beaten until thick, the melted chocolate, the flour, the extracts, and the stiffly beaten whites of the eggs.

Pour over the fruit and bake for half an hour in a very slow oven. Allow to become cold before cutting into neat squares. Pack in boxes between layers of waxed paper.

This candy, like fruit-cake, improves with age. The fruit may be dates, raisins, figs, pineapple, ginger, cherries, or whatever is available. Variety may easily be secured by putting different fruits on each quarter of the pan

CARAMEL FUDGE

1½ lbs. (3 cups) sugar   1 tablespoonful chopped an-
½ pint (1 cup) milk   gelica
1 teaspoonful vanilla extract

Caramelize one cupful of the sugar. Boil the milk and the remaining sugar, and when boiling, add the caramel sugar; stir constantly until it forms a soft ball when tried in cold water, or until it registers 240° by the thermometer; then remove from the fire, add the chopped angelica and the vanilla extract. Beat until creamy, and pour into buttered tins.

CHILDREN'S FUDGE

1 lb. (2 cups) sugar   ¼ lb. (1 cup) chopped nut
½ pint (1 cup) sour cream   meats
Pinch of salt   4 tablespoonfuls chopped
3 tablespoonfuls cocoa   ginger
1 gill (½ cup) water   1 oz. (2 tablespoonfuls) but-
½ teaspoonful ginger extract   ter

Cook the butter, sugar, cream, and salt until it comes to a boil; then add the cocoa made into a paste with the water, and cook until it forms a soft ball when tried in cold water, or registers 240° by the thermometer. Remove from the fire, and stir in the extract, nuts, and ginger.

Beat until creamy. Pour into buttered tins, and when cool, cut into squares, cubes, or diamonds. Do not beat too long or a gloss will not form on the top.

CHOCOLATE EGG FUDGE

½ lb. (1 cup) brown sugar
½ lb. (1 cup) granulated sugar
½ pint (1 cup) cream
2 ozs. (4 tablespoonfuls) butter
1 tablespoonful golden syrup

2 squares grated unsweetened chocolate
1 teaspoonful glucose
1 white of egg
2 teaspoonfuls vanilla extract

Boil the sugars, cream, glucose, syrup, and chocolate, stirring all the time, till the mixture reaches 250°, or forms a hard ball when tried in cold water.

Remove from the fire, add the vanilla extract and the butter, and beat until slightly cooled. Now add the stiffly beaten white of egg and beat the mixture until it becomes thick and creamy.

Pour at once into a buttered tin. Mark into squares when cool.

CHOCOLATE AND NUT FUDGE

1½ lbs. (3 cups) sugar
½ pint (1 cup) milk
1½ squares chocolate
1 oz. (2 tablespoonfuls) butter
Pinch of salt
Pinch cream of tartar

¼ lb. (1 cup) chopped nut meats
1 teaspoonful vanilla extract
1 teaspoonful coffee extract
1 tablespoonful chopped angelica

4

Boil the sugar, milk, chocolate, butter, salt, and cream of tartar until the syrup forms a soft ball when tried in cold water, or registers 240° by the thermometer. Remove from the fire and set in a cool place. When it begins to harden, place on a baking-board and knead until creamy, adding the extracts, angelica, and nut meats; then roll lengthwise and cut in slices.

COCOA FUDGE

2 ozs. (½ cup) cocoa	1 gill (½ cup) milk
1¼ lbs. (2½ cups) sugar	1 tablespoonful glucose
1 teaspoonful vanilla extract	1½ ozs. (3 tablespoonfuls)
2 tablespoonfuls fondant	butter

Put the sugar, glucose, butter, cocoa, and milk into a saucepan, and stir till it boils to 240°, or until it forms a soft ball when tested in cold water.

Remove from the fire, stir in the vanilla extract and the fondant. Beat till creamy and pour into a well-buttered pan.

When firm, cut in squares or bars.

COFFEE FUDGE

1 lb. (2 cups) sugar	¼ lb. (1 cup) broken shell-
½ pint (1 cup) strong coffee	bark or pecan-nut meats
½ oz. (1 tablespoonful) but-ter	½ teaspoonful almond ex-tract

Mix the sugar, coffee, and butter together in a saucepan and boil, stirring all the time, until the mixture reaches 240°, or forms a soft ball when tried in cold water.

Remove from the fire, add the almond extract, and beat until it begins to stiffen. Pour over the nuts in a buttered tin.

COLLEGE FUDGE

1 lb. (2 cups) sugar
½ pint (1 cup) cream
1 oz. (2 tablespoonfuls) butter
1 teaspoonful vanilla extract
2 ozs. (½ cup) chopped nut meats
1 tablespoonful chopped candied pineapple
1 tablespoonful chopped preserved ginger
1 tablespoonful chopped preserved cherries
1 square melted chocolate

Put the sugar, cream, and butter into a saucepan and boil for half an hour, stirring constantly; then add the chocolate and allow to boil up again. Remove from the fire and beat till creamy; then add the vanilla extract, the fruits, and the nut meats.

Pour into buttered tins and mark into squares when half cold.

DATE FUDGE

¼ lb. (1 cup) stoned dates
½ lb. (1 cup) granulated sugar
½ lb. (1 cup) brown sugar
1 gill (½ cup) cream
1 oz. (2 tablespoonfuls) butter
1 teaspoonful lemon extract
1 teaspoonful vanilla extract
1 tablespoonful glucose

Put the cream, sugars, butter, and glucose into a saucepan and cook slowly, stirring all the time, till the syrup reaches 240°, or forms a soft ball when tried in cold water. Remove the pan from the fire, add the dates cut in small pieces, and the extracts. Stir until creamy, and pour into buttered pans. When nearly cool, cut into squares.

Fig or cocoanut fudge may be made in the same way. Two chopped preserved or fresh peaches may be added instead of the dates.

DIVINITY FUDGE

½ lb. (1 cup) brown sugar
⅓ lb. (1 cup) granulated sugar
½ pint (1 cup) maple syrup
1 tablespoonful vinegar
1 teaspoonful glucose
1 teaspoonful rose extract
½ lb. (1 cup) maple-sugar
1 gill (½ cup) water

2 whites of eggs
¼ lb. (1 cup) chopped walnut meats
¼ lb. (1 cup) chopped pecan-nut meats
1 teaspoonful almond extract
½ pint (1 cup) water

Put the brown sugar, maple-sugar, vinegar, glucose, and water into a saucepan and boil, stirring all the time to 290°, or until it hardens when tested in cold water; remove from the fire and add the rose extract. Put the granulated sugar and the half cupful of water into another saucepan and boil to 240°, or until it forms a soft ball when tried in cold water.

Then pour gently into the stiffly beaten whites of the eggs, add the almond extract, and stir in the first boiling. Beat until it is creamy; then add the nut meats, and pour into buttered tins.

When firm, turn out and cut into squares.

FLUFFY RUFFLES FUDGE

1 lb. (2 cups) sugar
1 gill (½ cup) glucose
1 gill (½ cup) water
2 whites of eggs

¼ lb. (1 cup) chopped black-walnut meats
½ teaspoonful clove extract

Mix the sugar, glucose, and water together in a saucepan and boil to 290°, or until it will crack when tested in cold water. Pour on to the beaten whites of eggs, and beat until the mixture is stiff, but not too stiff to pour.

Add the extract and the nuts, and pour into a buttered tin. Press out flat with a buttered knife.

FIG AND RAISIN FUDGE

1½ lbs. (3 cups) sugar
½ pint (1 cup) milk
1 teaspoonful orange extract
¼ lb. (1 cup) chopped figs
¼ lb. (1 cup) chopped raisins

½ lb. (2 cups) chopped nut meats
1 oz. (2 tablespoonfuls) butter

Boil the sugar and milk together until it forms a soft ball when tried in cold water, or until it registers 240° by the thermometer; then add the butter, orange extract, fruits, and nut meats.

Remove from the fire, and stir until creamy; spread on buttered tins and cut into fancy shapes when cold.

HONEY CHERRY FUDGE

10 tablespoonfuls strained honey

10 tablespoonfuls cream

Pinch of salt

½ teaspoonful lemon-juice

Few preserved cherries

1 tablespoonful chopped candied citron peel

Bring the cream and the honey slowly to boiling-point; then cook for six minutes after the mixture begins to boil, or until a white line appears around the edge when the candy is stirred.

Remove at once from the fire, stir in the salt and the lemon-juice. Arrange the cherries on buttered pans, and pour the hot fudge over them. ·

Sprinkle over with the chopped peel.

MARSHMALLOW CHOCOLATE FUDGE

¼ lb. (1 cup) marshmallows

1 lb. (2 cups) sugar

½ pint (1 cup) cream

1 oz. (2 tablespoonfuls) butter

1 teaspoonful vanilla extract

3 tablespoonfuls grated chocolate or cocoa

Put the sugar, cream, and chocolate or cocoa into a saucepan, and when boiling, add the butter. Boil until when tried in cold water it forms a soft ball, or registers 240° by the thermometer. Remove from the fire, add the vanilla extract and the marsh-mallows (having broken each into three pieces).

Beat until thick, and pour into a buttered pan. Cut into squares when cool.

MARSHMALLOW FUDGE

½ lb. (2 cups) marshmallows   ½ pint (1 cup) water

1 lb. (2 cups) brown sugar   Pinch cream of tartar

½ lb. (1 cup) maple-sugar   1 tablespoonful chopped nut meats

Dissolve the sugars in the water, then add the cream of tartar, and boil without stirring until it registers 240°; or when tried in cold water it forms a soft ball. Remove from the fire, add the marshmallows broken into small pieces, and the nut meats.

Beat until it begins to stiffen; then pour into buttered tins.

MAPLE AND MARSHMALLOW FUDGE

½ pint (1 cup) maple syrup   1 teaspoonful vanilla extract

1 lb. (2 cups) granulated sugar   ½ teaspoonful lemon extract

1 gill (½ cup) cream   Marshmallows, whole or cut

1 oz. (2 tablespoonfuls) butter

Put the maple syrup, sugar, cream, and butter into a saucepan; stir constantly over the fire to 240°, or until, when tested in cold water, it forms a soft ball.

Remove from the fire, add the extracts, and beat until it begins to granulate.

Place some fresh marshmallows on a buttered pan and cover with the mixture.

When partly cool, cut in squares.

MAPLE FUDGE

1 lb. (2 cups) grated maple-sugar

½ pint (1 cup) milk

½ lb. (2 cups) chopped walnut or pecan-nut meats

1 oz. (2 tablespoonfuls) butter

½ lb. (1 cup) granulated sugar

1 teaspoonful vanilla extract

Put the maple-sugar and the milk into a saucepan and allow the mixture just to come to boiling-point without stirring.

Into another saucepan put the granulated sugar, and stir until it is brown; then pour in the maple-sugar and the milk; add the butter and boil, stirring all the time until it forms a soft ball when tried in cold water, or reaches 240°.

Remove from the fire, add the vanilla and the extracts. Beat until it is creamy. Pour into buttered tins or between buttered candy bars. Cut in squares and wrap in waxed paper when cold.

MAPLE NUT FUDGE

½ lb. (1 cup) maple-sugar

½ lb. (1 cup) brown sugar

1 oz. (2 tablespoonfuls) butter

1½ gills (¾ cup) golden syrup

2 squares chocolate

2 ozs. (½ cup) chopped nut meats

2 ozs. (½ cup) chopped cocoanut

1½ gills (¾ cup) cream

Put the sugars, butter, syrup, chocolate, and cream into a saucepan; cook, stirring all the time, until the syrup registers 240°, or until, when tested in cold water, it forms a soft ball.

Remove from the fire and beat until creamy; then pour into buttered tins, sprinkle the nuts over the top, and mark into squares when half cold.

NUT FUDGE

½ lb. (1 cup) brown sugar
1 gill (½ cup) milk
¼ lb. (1 cup) chopped nut meats
Pinch of salt
1 teaspoonful lemon extract
Pinch cream of tartar

½ lb. (1 cup) granulated sugar
1 gill (½ cup) cream
1 square grated chocolate
1 teaspoonful vanilla extract
2 tablespoonfuls chopped cherries

Put the brown sugar and milk into a saucepan and bring to boiling-point; then add the cream of tartar, and boil until it forms a soft ball when tried in cold water. Remove from the range, add the lemon extract, salt, and nut meats, beat till creamy, and pour into a deep buttered tin.

Put the granulated sugar and cream into a saucepan, and bring to boiling-point; add the chocolate and stir until it forms a soft ball when tried in cold water, or registers 240° by the thermometer; remove from the fire, add the vanilla extract and the cherries. Beat until creamy and pour over first part.

Cool and cut into bars or cubes.

This fudge may be dipped in melted flavored fondant.

PECAN FUDGE

1 lb. (2 cups) sugar
½ pint (1 cup) water
Pinch cream of tartar
¼ lb. (1 cup) chopped pecan-nut meats

1 oz. (2 tablespoonfuls) butter
3 tablespoonfuls fondant
1 teaspoonful vanilla extract

Dissolve the sugar in the water in a saucepan, add the cream of tartar, and boil until it registers 240°, or until, when tested in cold water, it forms a soft ball. Add the butter, fondant, chopped nuts, and vanilla extract. Remove from the fire, and beat until it begins to grain. Pour quickly into greased tins.

When cold, cut in squares and wrap in waxed paper.

TRILBY FUDGE

1 lb. (2 cups) sugar
1 can condensed milk
1 oz. (2 tablespoonfuls) butter
½ pint (1 cup) cream
2 teaspoonfuls golden syrup

Pinch cream of tartar
Few drops red color
1 tablespoonful chopped candied pineapple
½ teaspoonful pineapple extract

Put the butter, syrup, cream, and condensed milk into a saucepan, and dissolve over gentle heat, stirring all the time; then add the sugar and dissolve it, and finally add the cream of tartar.

Allow to boil till it forms a soft ball when tested in cold water, or registers 240° by the thermometer. Add the chopped pineapple, pineapple extract, and the red color, and boil till it forms a hard ball when tested in cold water, or registers 252° by the thermometer. Remove the pan to the table, and stir till it begins to grain; then pour quickly into well-buttered tins, and when half cold, score with a knife into neat squares. When cold, break apart.

PEANUT BUTTER FUDGE

2 heaping tablespoonfuls peanut butter
1 gill (½ cup) milk
1 lb. (2 cups) sugar
1 teaspoonful ginger extract

Put the sugar, milk, and peanut butter into a saucepan and stir until the mixture boils for exactly five minutes; remove from the fire, add the ginger extract, and stir until it thickens.

Pour into a buttered tin and cut when cold.

If liked, shelled and chopped roasted peanuts may be sprinkled on the pan before the mixture is turned in.

PRINCESS FUDGE

¾ lb. (1½ cups) sugar
1 oz. (2 tablespoonfuls) butter
3 squares of grated unsweetened chocolate
Pinch of salt
Pinch of baking soda
Pinch of powdered cinnamon
1 teaspoonful vanilla extract
½ teaspoonful lemon extract
½ pint (1 cup) milk

Put the milk, sugar, salt, soda, cinnamon, and chocolate into a saucepan; dissolve slowly, stir once, then boil gently until the syrup reaches 240°, or forms a soft ball when tried in cold water. Remove from the fire, add the extracts and the butter, and pour quickly on to a buttered slab or platter. When perfectly cold, beat with a wooden spoon until stiff enough to hold together; flatten out with a buttered knife, and cut into bars.

RASPBERRY NUT FUDGE

¼ lb. (⅓ cup) raspberry jam

½ teaspoonful raspberry extract

½ pint (1 cup) water

Few drops red color·

Pinch cream of.tartar

¼ lb. (1 cup) chopped black-walnut meats

1 lb. (2 cups) sugar

Dissolve the sugar in the water over a moderate fire, then add the cream of tartar, and boil to 245°, or till it forms a firm ball when tried in cold water. Pour the syrup into a wet basin, allow to stand for eight minutes, then add the raspberry jam (which should have been rubbed through a sieve and warmed), a few drops of red color, and the raspberry extract. Beat until it begins to grain; then add the nuts, and pour at once into a buttered tin. Mark into squares when cool.

SORORITY FUDGE

2 ozs. (¼ cup) butter

½ lb. (1 cup) brown sugar

½ lb. (1 cup) granulated sugar

1 gill (½ cup) cream

3 tablespoonfuls molasses

2 squares grated chocolate

1½ teaspoonfuls orange extract

4 tablespoonfuls chopped angelica

Mix the sugars, molasses, and cream in a saucepan, then add the butter, melted. Bring to a boil, and boil for three minutes, stirring rapidly. Add the chocolate, boil for five minutes, stirring quickly, then more slowly.

Remove from the fire, add the orange extract and the angelica. Stir until it thickens; then pour into buttered tins.

SOUTHERN FUDGE

1 gill (½ cup) water
1 gill (½ cup) golden syrup
¼ lb. (1 cup) chopped preserved ginger
1 white of egg

2 tablespoonfuls ginger
syrup
1 lb. (2 cups) confectioners'
sugar

Put the golden syrup, water, ginger syrup, and sugar into a saucepan, and boil, stirring all the time, to 240°, or until, when tested in cold water, it forms a soft ball.

Then pour on to the stiffly beaten white of egg, beating all the time, and beat till creamy. Add the ginger, and pour into a buttered tin.

When cold, cut into bars.

SULTANA AND NUT FUDGE

1½ ozs. (3 tablespoonfuls)
butter
¼ lb. (½ cup) chopped walnut meats
¼ lb. (1 cup) sultana raisins

1 teaspoonful vanilla extract
1 teaspoonful orange extract
1 gill (½ cup) milk
3 tablespoonfuls molasses
¾ lb. (1½ cups) sugar
3 squares chocolate

Put the butter, molasses, chocolate, sugar, and milk into a saucepan and stir over the fire until the mixture reaches 240°, or until, when tried in cold water, it forms a soft ball. Add the chopped nuts, raisins, and extracts, and remove from the fire. Beat until creamy; pour into buttered tins, and when cool, cut in neat squares.

FUDGE WITH WHIPPED CREAM

1½ lbs. (3 cups) brown sugar
½ pint (1 cup) milk
¼ lb. (½ cup) butter
Pinch of salt

¼ lb. (1 cup) chopped walnut meats
½ pint (1 cup) whipped cream
1 teaspoonful vanilla extract
½ square chocolate

Put the sugar into a saucepan, add the milk, butter, salt, and chocolate, and boil to 245°, or till the mixture hardens when tried in cold water. Remove the pan from the fire, and beat for three minutes with a wire egg-beater. Now add the cream and continue to beat; add the nuts and the vanilla extract.

Beat until almost cold, and pour into buttered tins to cool.

When quite cold, mark in squares.